CCSS Genre Biography

**Essential Question**
How does technology lead to creative ideas?

**SNAPSHOT!**
THE STORY OF GEORGE EASTMAN
BY JULIA WALL

These days, taking a photograph is easy. Most people use digital cameras. You can look at the photo right away. If you don't like it, you can take another one!

Printing digital images is easy, too. You can print them at home or you can take them to a store to print. Today's cameras are small, light devices. Many people own one.

Today most cell phones have a digital camera.

George Eastman began taking photographs in 1878. In those days, things were different. Photography took a lot of time and was also expensive. Images were made on heavy glass or metal plates, and they were **developed** using chemicals in a darkroom.

George Eastman changed the way that people took photographs.

They were often blurred, and they couldn't be printed on paper.

Eastman had an inquiring mind, so he spent hours experimenting. His work helped to change photography from an expensive and difficult task into an everyday activity.

# CHAPTER 1

# A PACK-HORSE LOAD

George Eastman was born in 1854 in Waterville, New York. His father died when George was seven. George's mother found it hard to make ends meet, so when he was 14, George left school and got a job to help out.

When he was 24, Eastman bought some equipment so that he could take photographs. He also paid $5 for some photography lessons because he had become passionate about taking photographs.

Eastman would have used a camera like this one.

These photographers took pictures of the Civil War. They needed a wagon to carry the photographic equipment.

When Eastman first started taking photos, he had a lot of equipment to carry. He claimed the equipment was like a "pack-horse load." His camera was big, and he also had to carry a large **tripod**. The camera sat on the tripod to help keep the camera still so he could take a clear photo. He also took a heavy canvas tent and glass plates, glass tanks, chemicals, and water to develop the photographs.

Hulton–Deutsch Collection/CORBIS

Before he took each photo, Eastman went into a dark tent and put chemicals on a glass plate. This was known as a wet plate.

Eastman had to develop the glass plate quickly after taking a photograph. If it dried out, the photo would be ruined.

Eastman read that some photographers in England were using other chemicals, and they were able to develop dry plates. Eastman decided to try to use the **formula** for one of these chemical mixtures to invent a better kind of photographic plate.

## THE WET-PLATE PROCESS

The photographer:

1 coated a glass plate with chemicals.

2 dipped the wet plate into a solution to make it sensitive to light.

3 put the wet plate into the camera.

4 took the photo.

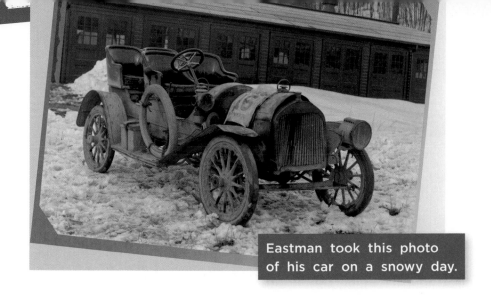

Eastman took this photo of his car on a snowy day.

Eastman tried different chemicals on the glass plates. Then he baked the plates in the oven to see how quickly they would dry.

Eastman did his experiments at night. During the day, he was working at a bank, so he was often very tired.

After more than two years, Eastman discovered a way to make a better dry plate. Then he invented a machine to coat the glass plates with chemicals. This meant he could make large numbers of dry plates and people would be able to buy them all ready to use.

In 1880, Eastman started his own business, selling his dry plates to photographers.

**STOP AND CHECK**

Why did Eastman invent dry plates?

# CHAPTER 2

# FROM GLASS TO PAPER

Although Eastman's plates made photography easier, the plates were made from glass and broke if they were dropped. Each plate could only hold one image, so taking more than one photo still took a lot of time.

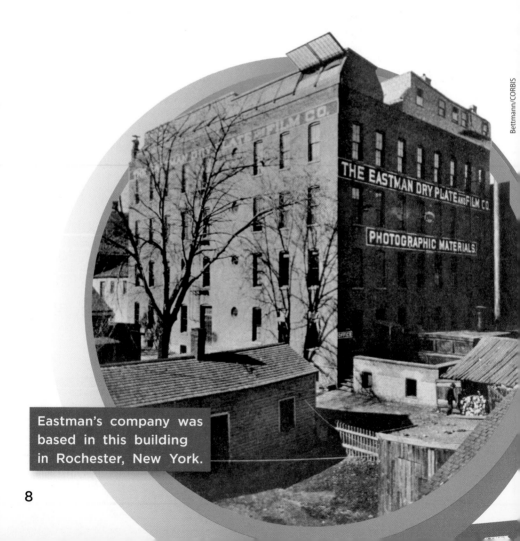

Bettmann/CORBIS

Eastman's company was based in this building in Rochester, New York.

Eastman knew he needed to find a better material than glass. He wanted something that wouldn't break easily. As well as having to be lighter and more flexible than glass, it also had to be able to take more than one photograph.

He decided to try paper. He wanted to coat it with something that was tough, yet flexible. His first experiments didn't work. Then, in 1884, Eastman was successful. He coated a roll of paper with chemicals and made a kind of film.

Next, Eastman began working on a way to put a roll of the paper film into a camera. An **engineer** named William Walker helped him.

Walker came up with an idea to use spools like the ones used on sewing machines. The film rolled from one spool to the other, and it could be used in any camera. In 1884, Walker and Eastman applied for patents for their film holder made of spools.

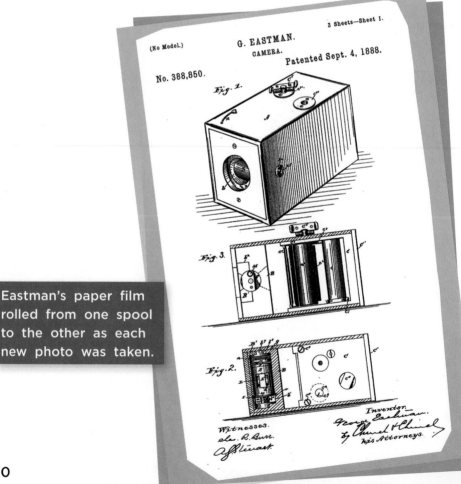

Eastman's paper film rolled from one spool to the other as each new photo was taken.

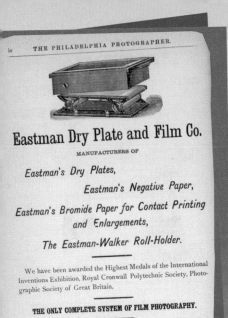

Eastman used advertising to help sell his inventions.

Eastman had invented film for cameras, but professional photographers weren't very interested in it. Pictures using the paper film weren't as clear as those using glass plates.

However, Eastman knew that people who took photos for a hobby wouldn't be as fussy. Those people wanted a camera that was simple to use.

Eastman envisioned a new kind of camera that would be easier to use. He wanted to get rid of the "pack-horse load." His new camera wouldn't need a tripod. It would be smaller and lighter, and could be held by hand. It would completely change photography.

**STOP AND CHECK**

Why was Eastman's camera easy to use?

# CHAPTER 3

# THE CONVENIENT CAMERA

Eastman worked hard on his new idea. The first of his new cameras went on sale in 1888. The **slogan** for the camera was "You press the button. We do the rest." When the film was finished, the photographer sent the camera to Eastman's factory in Rochester, New York. The film was developed and new film was put into the camera. Then Eastman's company sent the camera and the photographs back to the photographer.

When people tried the new cameras, they told others how easy they were to use. Word quickly spread and sales took off.

## EASTMAN'S CAMERA

Eastman's new camera cost $25. One roll of film could take 100 photos. The camera could take photos more quickly than other cameras.

**shutter:** controls the amount of light that is let in; the longer the shutter is open, the more light is let in

**lens:** allows light to be focused onto the film

Eastman wanted to make sure his company stayed one step ahead of the **competition**. He hired people to help, and this led to the next breakthrough: a camera for children.

The first children's camera was perfect for taking quick photos, or snapshots.

He began selling his children's camera in 1900. It only cost $1, so many could afford it. It was also very easy to use. Children were captivated. The camera was such a success that it was still being made in the 1950s.

**STOP AND CHECK**

Why was Eastman's children's camera so successful?

**case:** doesn't allow light into the camera

# CONCLUSION

Eastman came up with many new ideas for photography. He invented a type of dry plate, and then he invented paper film.

He also invented a hand-held camera. Photographers no longer needed to develop their own photographs. Finally, many people could afford to buy cameras and take photographs.

Eastman died in 1932. Since then, inventors have continued to improve photography with new ideas such as color film, instant cameras, and digital cameras. These modern advances have made taking snapshots more popular than ever.

# Respond to Reading

## Summarize

Use important details to summarize how Eastman's work with technology led to his creative ideas. Your graphic organizer may help you.

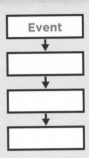

## Text Evidence

1. What kind of informational text is *Snapshot! The Story of George Eastman?* How do you know? GENRE

2. In Chapter 1, what things did Eastman do to invent dry glass plates? SEQUENCE

3. The Greek root *photo* means "light," and the root *graph* means "to write." How does knowing this help you understand the word *photograph*? GREEK ROOTS

4. Write about the steps Eastman took to invent film. WRITE ABOUT READING

**Compare Texts**
Read about how some boys use technology to choose the best outing for their mom's birthday.

# The
# Ultimate
# Birthday

"Look at this, Casey," says Charlie. Charlie is my twin brother. He's checking out party options on the Internet because Mom's birthday is on Friday. Dad said we could take her out to celebrate, but we can't agree on where to go.

"Take your loved one to the state fair," I read. "I don't think that would be Mom's thing, Charlie."

"How about you, Casey?" Dad inquires. "Do you have any ideas?"

"Yes, Mom would like to go bowling," I announce.

"Bowling!" groans Charlie. "When has Mom ever been bowling?"

16

Illustration: Mike Laughead

"Well, she likes trying out new things," I reply.

Charlie goes to another site. "Look," he exclaims enthusiastically, "here's an online poll about choosing your favorite car! A poll is a great way to compare things."

"Well, we could do an online poll and compare state fairs and bowling," I suggest.

"Great idea!" Dad agrees.

Charlie posts our ideas for Mom's birthday online, then he asks our friends and family to vote on which idea they like better.

People start commenting right away.

Our neighbor, Maddy, is first. "Charlie, I just can't see your mom cheering for a prize pig!" she writes.

"Casey, are you living in Dullsville?" That's from Mom's younger sister in Florida.

"Way to go, Aunt Becky!" laughs Charlie.

After three days, we look at the results. It's an even split! So we take Mom bowling AND to the state fair. And Mom being Mom, she says it's the best birthday ever.

## Make Connections

How do the twins use technology to agree on Mom's birthday outing? ESSENTIAL QUESTION

What was the role of technology in Eastman's inventions and in *The Ultimate Birthday*?
TEXT TO TEXT

Illustration: Mike Laughead

# Glossary

**competition** *(kom-pi-TISH-uhn)* a person or group you are trying to succeed against *(page 13)*

**developed** *(di-VEL-uhpt)* when film or a photographic plate is treated with chemicals so that a photographed image can be seen *(page 3)*

**engineer** *(en-juh-NEER)* a person who designs and builds things *(page 10)*

**formula** *(FOHR-myuh-luh)* a description of the ingredients that make up a substance *(page 6)*

**slogan** *(SLOH-guhn)* a short, persuasive phrase, often used in advertising *(page 12)*

**tripod** *(TRY-pahd)* a three-legged stand used to support and steady a camera *(page 5)*

# Index

# Focus on Science

**Purpose** To explore how technology leads to creative ideas

## Procedure

Scientists work to invent things when they have a problem they want to solve. They use a scientific process. First, they think of ideas that might solve the problem. Then they test their ideas by doing experiments.

**Step 1** With a partner, choose the invention of a technology that you would like to explore.

**Step 2** Research the invention, using the library or the Internet. Find out about the process scientists used that led to the invention.

**Step 3** Use the information you found to make a visual presentation or poster. Show the process the scientists used, and the invention. Share your presentation with the class.

**Conclusion** How might the invention you researched lead to even more exciting technology?